2 — THE NECESSITY TO P[ROVIDE] HARBOURS... THE IND[USTRY]

4 — THE MULBERRIES

8 — THE ELEMENTS THAT COMPRISED THE ARTIFICIAL HARBOURS

Gooseberries — 9
Bombardons — 10
Blockships — 11
Phoenix caissons — 12
Loebnitz platforms or unloading (spud) piers — 14
Floating causeways — 15

18 — FROM THEORY TO PRACTICE: INSTALLING THE HARBOURS

23 — THE UNEXPECTED CAPTURE OF OTHER PORTS ALONG THE NORMANDY COAST

24 — THE DEVASTATING STORM ON THE 19TH OF JUNE

27 — THE HARBOURS' LAST DAYS

32 — THE D-DAY MUSEUM

Zone tertiaire de Nonant - 14400 BAYEUX
Tel.: 02 31 51 81 31 – Fax: 02 31 51 81 32
info@orepeditions.com - www.orepeditions.com

Editor: Grégory PIQUE
Editorial coordination: Corine DESPREZ
Graphic design: Éditions OREP - Layout: Laurent SAND
Text by: Lieutenant Colonel Alain FERRAND

ISBN: 978-2-8151-0717-4 – © Éditions OREP 2024
All rights reserved - Legal deposit: 1st term 2004

THE INDISPENSIBLE SUPPLY CHAIN

The raid on Dieppe on 19th August 1942 comforted the Allies in their view that the Atlantic Wall was heavily defended at sites favourable to landings, particularly in the area around the Channel ports.

The capture of a fortified position on the French coast would therefore be costly in human lives and extremely difficult. To seize, intact, a port or harbour was a hope highly unlikely to be realized. Nevertheless, for an invasion to succeed, the Allies had an imperative need to acquire a means of landing and handling the tonnage of material and supplies required by a modern mechanised army, namely 40kg per man per day.

Arromanches beach on the eve of the 6th of June 1944.

During the Quebec Conference in July 1943, the plans devised via close collaboration between the British and American Chiefs of Staff for Allied strategic operations in North-West Europe in 1944 took shape, under the code name OVERLORD. These plans were to achieve the largest combination of air, land and naval operations known to history, with the dual purpose of supporting the Soviet Army in its struggle against the Nazi forces and the liberation of Western Europe.

The success of the landings and the remainder of the campaign would depend on the speed with which reinforcements and supplies could reach Normandy. With the support of air and naval forces, the Allies would need to land extensive land forces, under enemy fire, and to supply them with the essential reinforcements, equipment, food, war materials and supplies, once a bridgehead had been established, so that they could break out and advance into the heart of Europe to destroy the enemy's forces. To continuously supply the Allied forces from points on the beaches would be a high-risk operation, because bad weather, if combined with adverse tides, could lead to disaster and interrupt the flow of supplies.

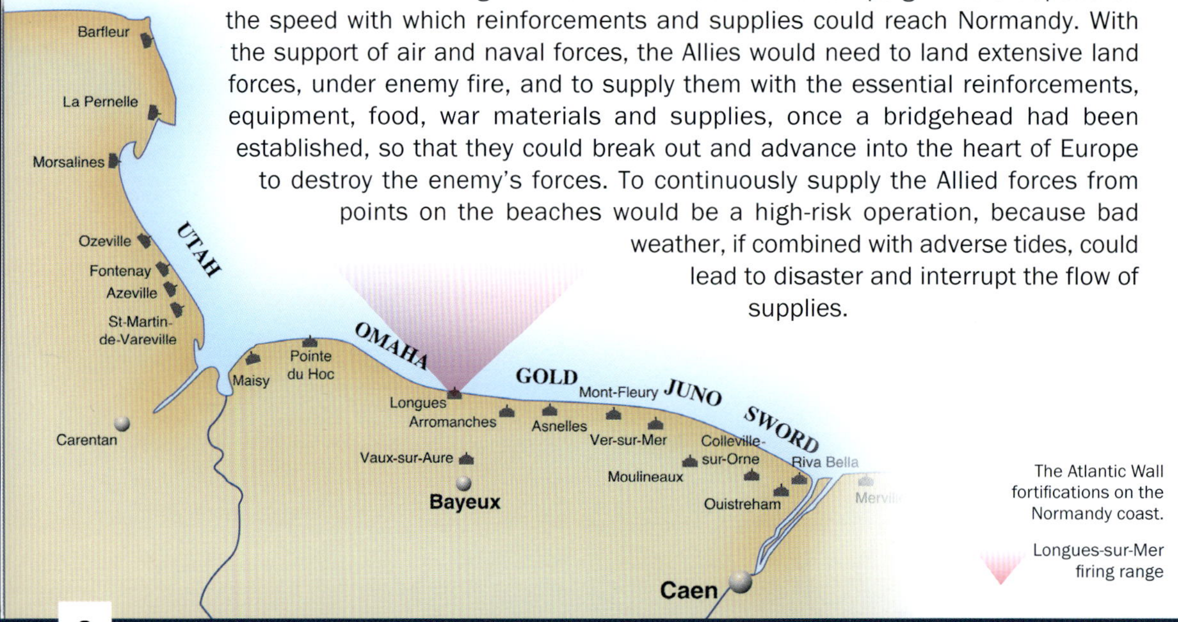

The Atlantic Wall fortifications on the Normandy coast.

Longues-sur-Mer firing range

Port Winston seen from the clifftop on the site of the Longues-sur-Mer German artillery battery.

Located about 6km west of Arromanches, the battery at Longues is an interesting example of coastal defence.

Its firing range extended over a large area of the Bay of Seine. Its four 152mm guns could hit a target at a distance of 20km.

Situated around 350m from the gun emplacements and 65m above sea level, on top of the cliffs, the command post comprised two floors.

- The lower floor, which was partially underground, housed the observation station, with a viewing slit extending over an arch of more than 180°.

- The upper floor was protected by a concrete roof slab supported on four small steel columns and contained the range-finding equipment needed to determine the distance from the target. The co-ordinates were transmitted to the gunners by telephone.

One of the Longues-sur-Mer battery casemates with its gun still in place.

The battery's command post.

It was therefore imperative to be able to land supplies without being subjected to such natural obstacles. The answer was to build a prefabricated port or harbour in England and to tow it across the Channel, install it and bring it into service with all possible speed.

To maintain an infantry division to challenge the enemy would require supplying it with 300 to 400 tonnes each day; an armoured division would need 1,200 tonnes. During the early stages of the invasion, given the size of the forces deployed, the supplies requiring to cross the Channel would amount to between 8,000 and 12,000 tonnes per day, without taking into account the need for forces to consolidate on the bridgeheads. Following this phase, the daily requirements would grow, month by month, by between 1,000 and 2,000 tonnes.

During an amphibious operation, there is always a critical period during which the initial waves of assault troops are exhausted. If the men from back-up and consolidation forces are not speedily brought in, or are inadequate in strength or in supplies, this critical period can be prolonged, hence jeopardising the success of the operation. This critical period starts on the second day of an operation.

Once the beaches had been won, the Allies needed to quickly reinforce their forces in the narrow beachhead, before Rommel's troops could reach the battlefield. Under these conditions, port facilities were essential for supplying land forces.

THE MULBERRIES

The SHAEF (*Supreme Headquarters Allied Expeditionary Force*). From left to right: General Bradley, Admiral Ramsay, Air Chief Marshal Tedder, General Eisenhower, General Montgomery, Air Chief Marshal Leigh Mallory and General Bedell-Smith

The initial objective of the landing was to secure a wide bridgehead comprising Brittany and a share of Normandy, from the Seine to the Loire and ending at a line from Rouen to Orléans. It was not to engage in a pitched battle to destroy the German Army in the West. This latter objective was only to be achieved during the second week of August, when the Allied armies trapped the Germans in the Falaise pocket.

During the first phase, from D-Day to D-Day + 17, the military plan envisaged taking Cherbourg and the Cotentin Peninsula and covering its Calvados flank to the east of Caen. During the second phase, the Allies would hold Caen to guard their left flank and would then move from the Cotentin towards Rennes and Nantes, to isolate the Brittany peninsula. This operation was to be completed by the thirtieth day. The third phase was to last for two months and consisted in liberating the Brittany peninsula up to the Loire, organising a naval base in Quiberon Bay (Operation CHASTITY), then extending the Normandy bridgehead eastwards as far as the Seine, and to the southeast, as far as the Nantes-Orléans line.

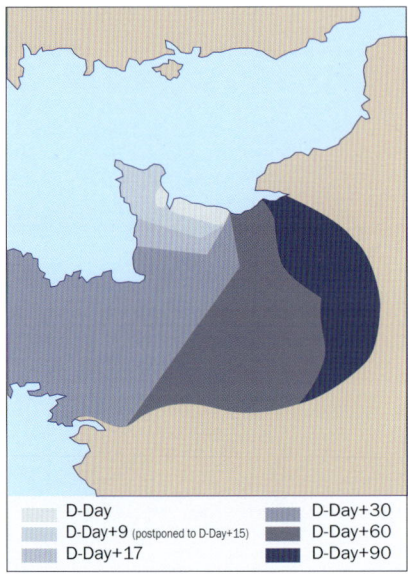

D-Day
D-Day+9 (postponed to D-Day+15)
D-Day+17
D-Day+30
D-Day+60
D-Day+90

Forecast Allied troop advance at D-Day + 90 days.

It was only after three months that, based on this wide bridgehead, the Allied armies were to be reinforced - the British via Cherbourg and the Americans via a base to be created in Morbihan Bay - before pushing eastwards towards the heart of Germany, ready for the decisive battle that would end the War.

From the start, we can see the vital importance attached to ports, whose capture was clearly essential to the success of large-scale operations. But pending the capture of Cherbourg and the subsequent operations, it was going to be absolutely essential to provide the invasion troops with the necessary supplies without which any attempt at landing in France would be doomed to failure. As the invasion progressed, it diverted from the intended plan. It took 80 days to reach the Seine and then 20 days in pursuit of the enemy before the front was stabilised. However, by the 12th of September, no German combatants remained in Normandy (except for those taken prisoner).

Landing craft were intended to beach themselves on the shore and discharge men and war materials; however, the Royal Navy considered that frequent beaching would damage the bases of these craft and that this method of landing men and materials should therefore be reserved for assault operations and not for supply missions. Moreover, beaching was a time-consuming operation because it was necessary to wait for the next favourable tide for the vessel to be refloated.

Furthermore, the number of troop landing craft (LCT), as well as their tonnage, was limited and the use of cargo ships and coasters appeared to be essential. However, a 2,000 tonne ship cannot approach an open Normandy shore closer than 1 nautical mile. In addition, to speed up turnaround and to achieve a continuous flow of supplies, it would be essential to unload them directly onto the lorries that would transport supplies to the troops.

Construction of a Loebnitz platform.

Finally, even if it were possible for troops to be landed relatively quickly from beached landing craft, to achieve the same efficiency in the unloading of vehicles and supplies required for the frontline troops, it would be necessary to have available quays and ship discharge facilities. In these circumstances, and in the absence of any certainty that an existing port could be seized by force, the construction of artificial port and harbour facilities became a matter of vital importance.

As early as 1941, Churchill had instructed Admiral Mountbatten to develop amphibious warfare techniques and to investigate the possibilities for installing unloading quays on beaches.

On 30th May 1942, the British Prime Minister wrote a memorandum to Mountbatten regarding the qualities of floating quays and jetties. Thereafter, in

Construction of Phoenix caissons.

Construction and assembly sites and towing itineraries for the elements that comprised the artificial harbours.

the greatest secrecy, a team under the designation "Transportation 5" or "Tn.5", was entrusted with the responsibility of designing port structures. Answers to the associated issues only began to emerge after Churchill started to take a personal interest in the subject, making it clear in a circular, that was later to become famous, that he would tolerate no delay ("Bring me the best solution; do not waste time talking about the problems, these will look after themselves."). It was on the occasion of the "Rattle" Conference, held in Scotland on the 2nd and 3rd of July 1943 that, for the first time, the Allies brought up the question of artificial harbours and port facilities. Later in the month, this subject was to be examined in greater detail during the Quebec Conference, in the presence of Churchill and Roosevelt.

General Eisenhower, Commander in Chief of the Allied Forces and Admiral Sir B. Ramsay, commander of the Allied naval forces, took the view that until such time as existing French ports could be seized, OPERATION OVERLORD could not be completely accomplished without the use of artificial ports. Vice-Admiral W. G. Tennant was entrusted with the responsibility of all aspects pertaining to artificial harbours. On D-Day he was in command of more than 500 officers and around 10,000 men.

The harbour creation project as a whole was given the code name "Mulberry". This name was chosen at random, but later it was observed that mulberry trees grow rapidly in size, a happy omen for an enterprise which was rapidly to be brought to fruition. Speed was of the essence for the construction of these harbours. It was intended that their installation should be completed within two weeks and

Thousands of barges gathered in southern English ports.

View of *Mulberry B*'s floating causeway immediately after D-Day.

that they should have the capacity of the Port of Dover (Dover covered 310 hectares and, in 1944, would have allowed the discharge of 6,000 tonnes of supplies and 1,250 vehicles per day). However, its construction had taken seven years!

These harbours would serve a dual purpose:
- They would provide shelter for ships and particularly for flat-bottomed vessels such as landing craft.

- They would ease the landing of troops, vehicles and supplies of all kinds.
In their initial studies, the planners had assumed the landing of an assault force of 3 Divisions, increased to 10 Divisions as from D-Day+5 and followed by the landing of one Division per day. Based on this scenario, some 10,000 tonnes per day would be required on D-Day+3, 15,000 tonnes on D-Day+12 and 18,000 on D-Day+18. However, alterations to the plan of attack, made by the Commander in Chief early 1944, resulting in an increase in the D-Day assault force by two Divisions, substantially augmented forecast requirements.

Due to the great difficulty involved in towing enormous sections of artificial harbour across the Atlantic, it was decided that these harbour structures (*Mulberry A* for the Americans and *Mulberry B* for the British) would be built in Great Britain, despite the many problems this might cause, and that they would be towed across the Channel.

This picture shows the breakwater formed by the Phoenix caissons and *Blockships*, as well as the piers that were linked to the shore by floating causeways.

THE ELEMENTS THAT COMPRISED THE ARTIFICIAL HARBOURS

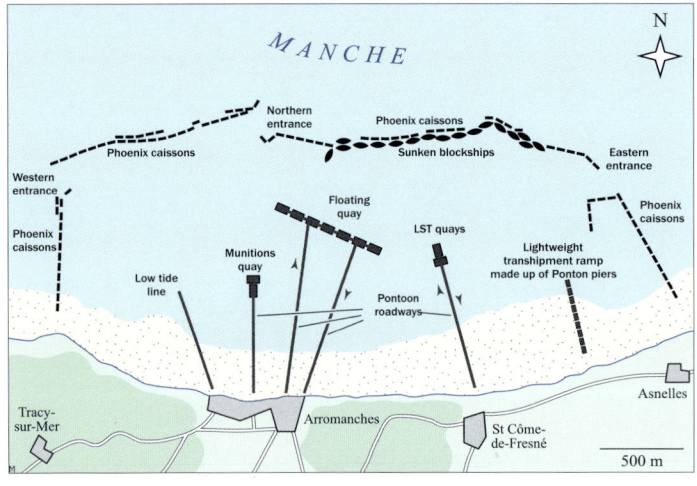

Simplified plan of *Mulberry B* at Arromanches. © Yann Magdelaine.

Each harbour would consist of:

- An outer, floating, breakwater comprised of "bombardons".

- An inner, fixed, breakwater consisting of concrete caissons and of ships expressly scuttled for this purpose, collectively known as *Gooseberries*.

- Floating jetties, extending from the beaches to jetty heads, mounted on stakes, against which ships could berth.

For technical reasons the concrete breakwater caissons could not be sunk in water deeper than 10 metres, but they would nevertheless enable coastal ships to use the inner harbour in calm water conditions whilst the larger "Liberty Ships" could unload in the rather less sheltered water behind the floating breakwaters.

The high water mark traditionally denotes the line of demarcation between the responsibilities of the British Navy and Army and, in consequence, although the responsibility for constructing the caissons was a matter for the War Office, it was the Navy that was responsible for getting them into position. In practice, it took a whole year to design and build all the elements that comprised the harbours. It was a major task and Churchill's personal intervention became necessary to resolve all the problems and to determine the priorities. At a period when all UK naval shipyards were fully

Protected by *Mulberry A's Gooseberry* on Omaha Beach.

occupied building landing craft, special basins had to be excavated along the banks of the Thames in which the Phoenix caissons could be built.

By the of 6th June, everything was ready. As the ships which were to form the rings of *blockships* set sail, the other harbour elements were prepared to be towed across the Channel by 132 tugs. The bombardons left first, followed, on the nights of the 6th and 7th of June, by the Phoenix caissons.

Aerial view of the Omaha Beach *Gooseberry* around the 15th of June 1944.

THE *GOOSEBERRIES*

Placed in position off the five invasion beaches (including those which would not comprise a "port"), in order to facilitate unloading operations, these were made up of floating elements, referred to as "bombardons" and sunken elements, "blockships" and, in addition, Phoenix caissons. They provided an area of sheltered water offshore from the beaches and thus allowed the berthing of landing craft and the unloading of ships.

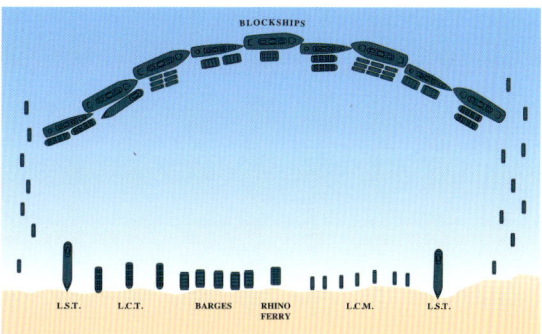
Standard plan of a *Gooseberry*.

Panoramic view of *Mulberry B* created with period pictures.

Theoretical diagram of a bombardon and of the line they collectively formed to break the waters when placed next to each other.

THE BOMBARDONS

Situated offshore of the artificial harbour structures, this first type of breakwater was composed of a chain of floating, cruciform-shaped, rafts. Each steel raft was 65m long, 8m high and had a draught of 6m. They were hollow and could be partially filled with water, but remained afloat thanks to watertight compartments. They were anchored in 20m of water and each was separated from its neighbour by 15 metres. Placed end to end, they formed a 1,600 metre-long barrier.

The bombardon was the application of a principle which had been discovered during the preliminary studies. It was found that when a wave hits a heavy, floating barrier, it loses a great deal of its energy. Thus, a 2 metre-high wave is reduced to 1 metre in the lee of the barrier.

Protected from the heaviest swells by the bombardons, large merchant ships whose draught prevented them from discharging their cargos in the inner harbour, could nevertheless acceptably transfer cargo to other suitable craft: DUKWs and *Rhinoferries*.

The Rhinoferry

These huge steel platforms, propelled by outboard motors, were used to transport standard and armoured vehicles between the ships and the beach. This type of raft weighed 400 tonnes and measured 60m by 15m. It was difficult to manoeuvre except in very calm seas. The freeboard was only 30cm. A large number were lost during the storm that struck mid-June. The elements that comprised them could be transported vertically on the sides of LSTs and they could then be assembled, according to requirements.

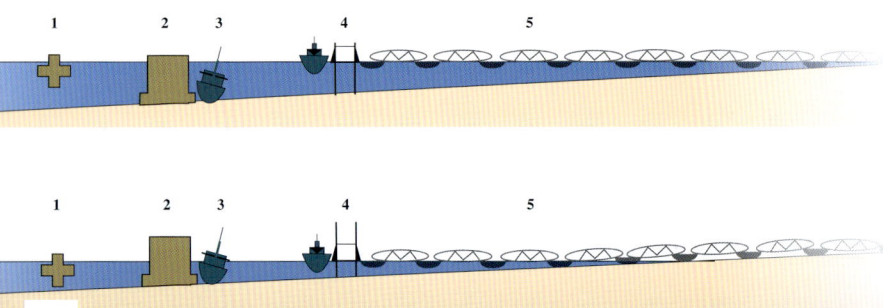

Theoretical diagram of an artificial harbour working in time with the tide thanks to cable reels.
1. Bombardon
2. Phoenix caisson
3. Blockship
4. Loebnitz platform
5. Floating causeway

Rhinoferries provided a link between the large ships out at sea and the beaches.

BLOCKSHIPS

The ability to sink old ships to form breakwaters was a considerable advantage in that the ships could move into position under their own power, hence economising tug resources, which were limited and already extremely in need both for towing the harbour elements across the Channel and installing them, and for satisfying existing needs in British ports. For the scuttling organised on the 7th of June off the landing beaches, at a depth of 5 metres at low tide, obsolete warships and merchant ships with a height from keel to upper deck of at least 12 metres were chosen; this meant that at high tide, a minimum of two metres would be above water. As such, they collectively comprised a mole, a continuous protective wall around the artificial harbour, and provided sheltered water for the unloading operations which needed to be launched as soon as possible, without waiting for the entire harbour to become operational. They would also provide shelter for smaller ships during high winds and storms. In addition, it became clear that the upperworks of these ships could be used as administrative quarters, for first aid care, as repair shops and as living quarters for the crews of the barges that ferried supplies between the large ships anchored offshore and the beaches.

Mulberry A's line of *blockships* opposite the Omaha sector.

In all, these old vessels collectively comprised some 7,000 metres of breakwater stretching over the five invasion beaches. Among them, the old French cruiser 'Courbet', scuttled off Sword beach, was able to render its last service to the Allies. We should not overlook, in this short historical account, that on the 7th of June, on Utah beach, the German coastal batteries were still operational during the construction of *Gooseberry* I. They successfully sank the second and third *blockships*. Nevertheless, happily, these ships went down in their intended positions, even if Radio Berlin announced this as a success by the German defenders!

A submerged *blockship*.

11

Turret mounted on a caisson and armed with an anti-aircraft gun.

Theoretical diagram of the immersion of a Phoenix caisson.

THE "PHOENIX" CAISSONS

The initial demand was for 147 caissons for both harbours. 212 were built up to the summer of 1944. They served to strengthen the harbour sea defences or were later used to repair certain ports which had been destroyed, such as Le Havre, and the sea wall at Walcheren in Holland.

Phoenix caisson being positioned in Arromanches artificial harbour.

Caisson filled with a mixture of sand and water (after submersion) to secure it. Technique referred to as "sand filling".

Six different sizes were required, depending on the sites where they were to be sunk (a task taking from 22 to 50 minutes according to conditions out at sea and requiring continuous monitoring and improvement). The largest weighed 6,044 tonnes and the smallest 1,672 tonnes. The largest were 60 metres long, 17 metres wide and 18 metres high. They collectively required 275,000 cubic metres of concrete, for a total weight of nearly 600,000 tonnes, 31,000 tonnes of steel and a million and a half square metres of corrugated sheet steel. Each caisson took 4 months to build.

Towed across the Channel by powerful tugs, the caissons were sunk off the shore along a contour line of a maximum depth of 9 metres. They comprised the backbone of the breakwaters that protected the harbours and completed the chain of breakwaters made up of *Gooseberries*. Each caisson comprised, in addition to a shelter for the crew during transit, a platform for mounting a Bofors anti-aircraft gun, with protection for its crew, and a hold for twenty tonnes of ammunition formed within the upper part of the structure. Contrary to what is sometimes asserted, it would appear that the caissons were not used to store fuel. No document relating to them makes any mention of this. One can see at least two good reasons why they should not have been used for this purpose; the caissons could only be held in position on the seabed if they were filled with seawater or sand. Had they been filled with fuel oil or other fuels at the time the other ships were being loaded in Great Britain, they would have become lighter and would have tended to float out of position, thus defeating their original purpose. Moreover, since the caissons

were exposed to the elements, rain and seawater would have contaminated the fuel, which would have caused problems.

The caissons sunk offshore had no decks. Others were sunk side by side at right angles to the shore, constituting shelter-jetties offering lateral protection to the harbour and serving as unloading quays for small ships.

Installation of a defensive turret.

The harbour in Arromanches was protected by a range of defensive systems: anti-aircraft guns installed on top of the Phoenix caissons, artificial fog and barrage balloons to prevent German planes from flying above.

Towing and installation of the *Mulberry B* unloading platforms at Arromanches.

"WHALE PIERS" OR "LOEBNITZ PIERS"

These berthing quays were concrete and steel pontoons of 1,100 tonnes deadweight. Rectangular in shape, they were fitted at each corner with square-section steel piles, of a length of 30 metres and a weight of 40 tonnes and sliding in specially-designed housings. Vertical movement of these piles was controlled by cable and pulley systems powered by large diesel engines.

Thanks to this ingenious system, they moved up and down in time with the ebb and flow of the tide and continuous unloading of ships was therefore ensured at all times. The interior of each structure comprised eighteen compartments providing technical service rooms, storage and quarters for the crew.

Floating causeways linked the spud piers with dry land. This one is at *Mulberry A* on Omaha Beach.

Scale model of the mooring piers, on display at the D-Day Museum in Arromanches.

To increase both the overall length and the unloading capacity of these quays, intermediate concrete structures were sunk between adjacent floating structures.

In addition, a further detail was incorporated within the floating quays, consisting of a sort of steel ramp which could be lowered slowly into the water. It was designed to allow the unloading of Landing Ship Tanks (LST). This system, to which a side platform was added, permitted simultaneous unloading from both decks of such vessels, hence saving considerable time. When an LCT was beached, the lower deck of the vessel was discharged first of all, then, by means of an internal hoist, the vehicles on the upper deck were brought down to the lower deck for unloading. At the same time, on the other sides of the floating quay, the cargo from coastal vessels could be unloaded directly onto waiting lorries.

FLOATING CAUSEWAYS

These were articulated steel structures designed to be mounted on steel or concrete caissons. At one end, they were fixed to the beach and at the other, to floating pontoons. Given the tidal range on this coast, the range of vertical movement of these elements could reach six metres whilst, at low water, the caissons rested on the sand. For both harbours, a total of eleven kilometres of flexible roadways were planned, as well as a special anchoring system to prevent them from oscillating and breaking up under the influence of the tidal currents. Depending on their intended use, these roadways could support 25 or 40 tonne armoured vehicles.

Originally designed to be built exclusively of steel, which was in very short supply at the time, many floaters (470 of a total of 670) were finally built of concrete. To do this, it was necessary to develop a concrete structure which was both strong and light, as well as being watertight and able to float. These floating structures were called "Beetles". Half a dozen of them can still be found on Arromanches beach.

The stud piers and floating causeways of the prefabricated harbour in Arromanches during the summer of 1944.

Cable reels enabled the floating causeways to be constantly kept at the right height, whatever the tide level.

Some steel caissons were employed in areas of rocky seabed where, closer to shore, concrete caissons would have been damaged. They had four small adjustable stilts incorporated within them. During their cross-Channel transport, these structures were towed in lengths of 150m, but proved to be particularly vulnerable to the elements, 50% of them being lost.

Adapting the beaches
It had to be possible to cross:
- the tidal belt of wet sand the consistency of which varied from hour to hour.
- the belt of dry sand above the high water mark, sometimes prolonged by dunes or cliffs in which breaches had been made by the Allied bombardment.
- behind the dunes or the cliffs, where there were marshy areas or a plateau with rare roads or paths which were unsuitable for the heavy traffic envisaged.

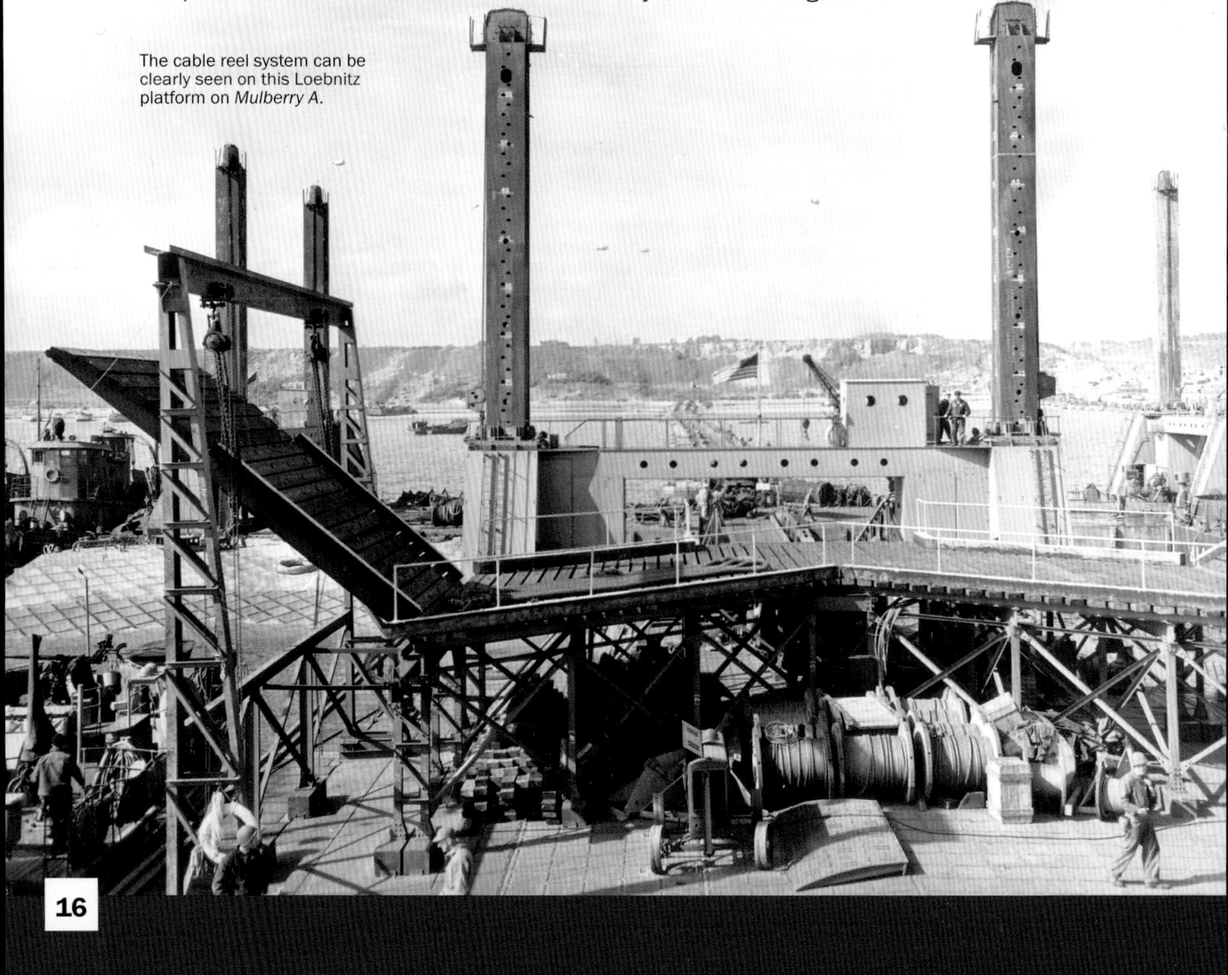

The cable reel system can be clearly seen on this Loebnitz platform on *Mulberry A*.

Floating causeway in the prefabricated harbour on Omaha Beach.

Three types of materials were available to create instant roadways:

• Prefabricated interlocking perforated metal sheets called PSPs; rolls of metal mesh of various shapes and strengths which could be unrolled and anchored to the ground (vestiges of which can still be found in the sand dunes at Utah beach).

• A surfacing material consisting of rolls of a natural fibre, coconut or raffia, which could be laid by a modified tank known as a "BOBIN" (a pun coined by the British General Hobart).

Floating causeway equipped with PSP metal surfacing.

• A surfacing material consisting of a felt impregnated with bitumen and called "Prefabricated Bituminous Surfacing". This zone was of capital importance for the British supply system. It was situated between the main base in Great Britain and the Army Corps maintenance areas. It occupied the whole zone to the south of Arromanches and the three British beaches, extending to the south of Bayeux and to the gates of Caen. Main roads linked this zone and the attacking forces' logistics units.

Securing a floating causeway to the unloading pier. The two floaters were used to adjust height.

Floating causeway comprised of metal spans mounted on "Beetle" floaters.

17

FROM THEORY TO PRACTICE: INSTALLING THE HARBOURS

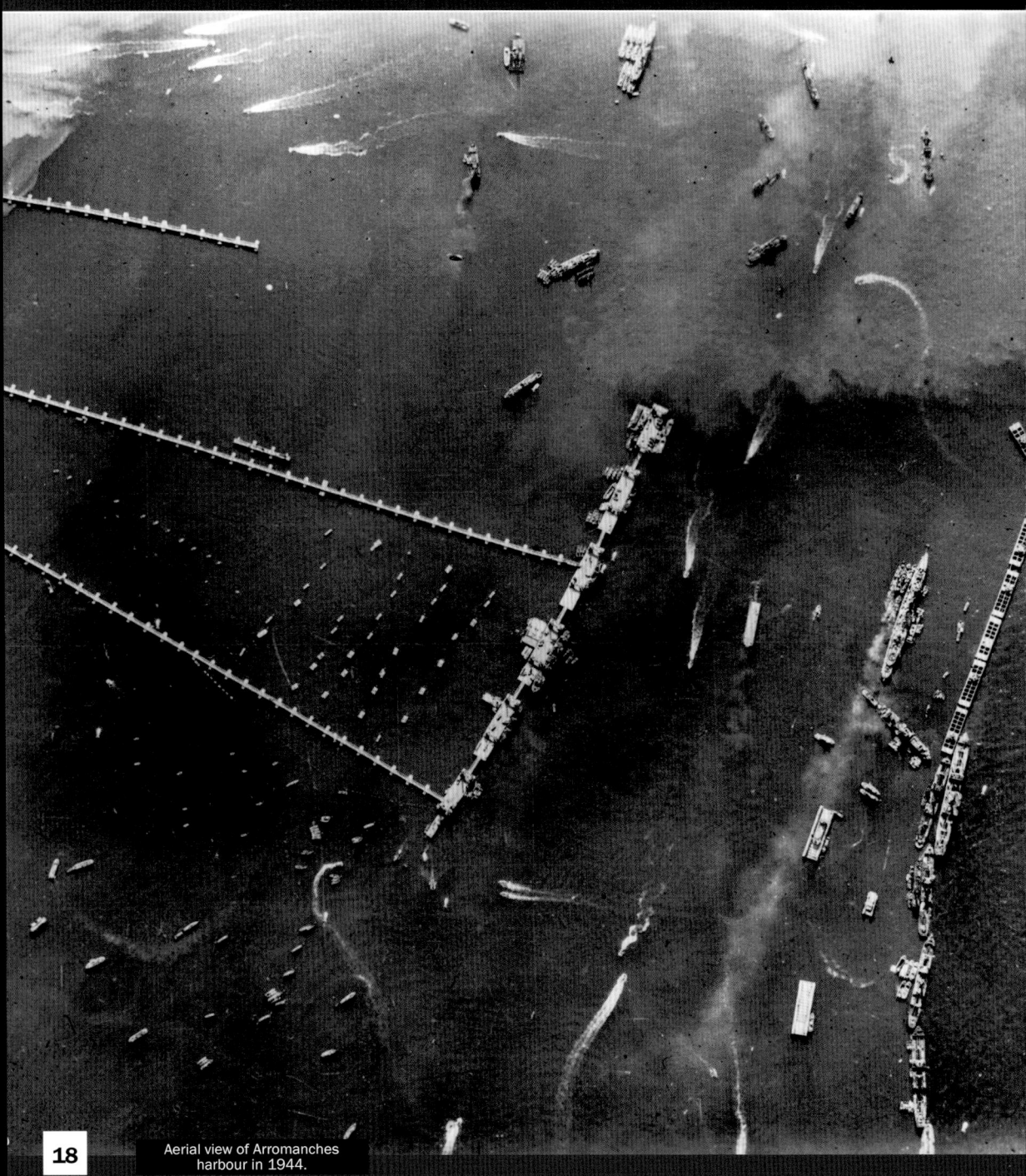

Aerial view of Arromanches harbour in 1944.

Light vehicle unloading operation at *Mulberry B*.

On D-Day, on the 6th of June, tugs towed the first elements of the artificial harbours towards the Normandy beaches. The ships destined to be scuttled to form *Gooseberries* had been prepared some hours earlier. They would be the first to arrive and, as from the 7th of June, would form an initial sheltered area which would facilitate the landings on each invasion beach.

During the night of D-Day/D-Day+1, Admiral Ramsay took a decision which was to have serious consequences during the storm that struck later in the month. To economise on tugs and on the manpower needed for other tasks, he decided to reduce the double line of bombardons, as originally proposed, to a single line. This would reduce the expected attenuation of the force of the swell. In addition, due to an error, the bombardons were placed in water of twice the originally-planned depth. On the 8th of June, the caissons arrived in sight of the beaches. On the 10th of June, *Mulberry A* already comprised 6 scuttled ships forming an initial breakwater, but only two Phoenix caissons and twelve bombardons had been anchored. This delay was due to enemy fire against the harbour area. At *Mulberry B*, the mole had been installed to the west of the north harbour entrance and a start had been made on the LST jetties. The work went on, night and day, under the protection of artificial fog. On the 11th of June, the *Gooseberries* were in position on the Utah, Omaha, Gold, Juno and Sword beaches. On the 17th of June, a vast share of the caissons which were to form the main breakwater of the artificial harbours was in place off the Normandy coast and the bombardons had been anchored in their final positions.

The same activity at *Mulberry A* on Omaha Beach.

At Arromanches, the east floating roadway of the future central quay had been in place since the 14th of June, with, at its extremity, a quay enabling coasters to unload directly onto supply lorries. The installation of the LST jetty was delayed, owing to the loss during transport of numerous sections of floating jetty, among which several units fitted with adjustable corner jacks. At St. Laurent, the first unloading station and its access road were already in service. On the 16th of June, the central jetty at *Mulberry A* was complete and linked to the berthing quay.

It appears that on this day, the Germans finally grasped the importance of the Mulberries and started to launch air attacks on them. They were defended by the Allied Air Forces and by anti-aircraft guns on the ships, the caissons and the beaches. Anti-aircraft balloons and smoke screens completed the defensive system. At Arromanches, with the Mayor's consent, the German seafront defences which hindered the exits from the harbour were destroyed.

At *Mulberry A*, the planned 24 bombardons had been anchored in position, 32 of the 51 Phoenix caissons were in place and moorings for two Liberty Ships were available. Three floating jetties were pending imminent completion and two of the six berthing quays on jack-up piles had been installed. The central quay, reserved for unloading LSTs, operated at the average rate of one LST per 64 minutes, i.e. one vehicle every 1 minute 16 seconds (instead of the 12 to 14 hours needed to unload and then wait for the next tide). Thereafter, all the troops landed at Omaha were able to do so without getting wet, across the floating roadway. Initial plans had not envisaged completion of *Mulberry A* before the 24th of June.

Installing the floating causeways.

At this stage, the harbour at Arromanches was closer to completion than the one in St. Laurent, since the British had tested assembly of major harbour elements late May – early June. The Americans were unable to prepare for their own elements had been delivered too late. In each artificial harbour, 115 barges and Rhinos and 100 DUKWs were at work discharging the

Unloading pier heads on stakes (spuds).

ships pending the installation of the floating quays that would enable direct unloading.

The harbour at Arromanches already provided a safe shelter for the small craft such as DUKWs and Rhinos which ensured the transportation of supplies between ship and shore. Once complete, the harbour was to provide:

- two floating quays, arranged in a T-shape and connected to land by a reinforced floating roadway for the landing of all vehicular equipment, (the east quay)

Unloaded vehicles heading for dry land.

- seven floating quays and their intermediate elements, connected to land by two jetties and enabling unloading to take place in an endless stream, as well as the embarkation of the wounded (the central quay)

- a special pontoon consisting of two floating quays linked together by a jetty and reserved solely for unloading ammunition (the west quay).

The combination of the several types of breakwater enabled the harbour at Omaha beach, *Mulberry A*, to provide the capacity to moor 7 Liberty Ships, 5 large coasters and 7 medium-sized coasters. Of its 3 berthing quays with floating jetty, the one reserved for unloading tanks had a capacity of 40 tonnes, and the other two 25 tonnes. The 6 berthing quays, which were grouped in twos, were able to accommodate either LSTs or coasters, or both.

Thus, the port could unload a daily tonnage of 5,000 and 1,400 vehicles. In addition, a floating roadway connected to the shore enabled LCTs and other landing craft (LCT = Landing Craft Tanks, of which there were 9 types, capable of transporting 3 to 8 heavy tanks or 250 to 300 tonnes of supplies) to unload directly from their holds. Only four Phoenix caissons were lost during the installation phase, two due to bad weather, one by hitting a mine and the last hit by a torpedo.

The floating causeways provided a link of just over half a mile between the unloading piers and dry land.

THE UNEXPECTED CAPTURE OF OTHER PORTS ALONG THE NORMANDY COAST

The capture of ports in the operational zone had been planned for, but it seemed probable that the Germans would have mined or destroyed them before the Allies could take them. Thus, the control of small but intact fishing harbours along the coast was very welcome.

One of them, Port-en-Bessin, situated at the junction between the American and British operational zones, was taken by the 47th Royal Marine Commando unit, by day on the 8th of June. As from the 12th, it enabled a total of 94,000 tonnes of supplies to be processed, a figure greatly in excess of volumes handled in times of peace. The harbour ceased operation on the 25th of September 1944. Another important port to be captured was that of Courseulles, in the Canadian Juno sector, to the east of Arromanches. Theoretically, this port should have been able to handle more than Port-en-Bessin. Unfortunately, due as much to the neglect of maintenance over the previous years as to the destruction caused by the Germans, it proved impossible to improve its handling capacity and from the 8th of June it was only capable of dealing with 1,000 tonnes per day.

Other small Normandy ports in Carentan, Grandcamp, Isigny, Barfleur and St. Vaast contributed their modest share to the unloading of coastal ships, although at low tide, they were of little use. Grandcamp and Isigny, restored to service, received their first cargoes on the 23rd of June, St. Vaast on the 9th of July, and Carentan and Barfleur on the 23rd of July.

During July, given the danger of insufficient unloading capacity (i.e. 17,000 tonnes per day), it was decided to expand as far as possible the handling capacity of these small ports. It was estimated that Carentan and Barfleur could, at full stretch, respectively handle 4,000 and 2,500 tonnes every day. The necessary dredging and infrastructure improvements began, but difficulties followed, one after another. So, Carentan was abandoned, after having worked for only from the 23rd to the 31st of July. At the latest, all these ports ceased to operate mid-October.

The metal caisson jetty at Courseulles protected by the *Gooseberry*.

THE DEVASTATING STORM ON THE 19TH OF JUNE

Unfortunately, at dawn on the 19th of June, all this fine planning and all the efforts deployed to ensure a continuous flow of reinforcements were brought to naught by a Force 6 to 7 storm of long-since unseen severity in those parts. Beginning with a stiff breeze from the northeast, the storm raged for three days, causing considerable damage and wreaking chaos along the Normandy coast. From the beginning of the storm, unloading operations were interrupted.

Arromanches during the storm.

Yet the storm was no surprise, for military planners had estimated that between May and September, stormy weather could occur for four successive days each month. Consequently, it had been planned to increase the daily unloading rate by 30% as from D-Day +4. However, what was surprising, was the sheer strength of the storm; some said that no similar conditions had been seen for forty years. The storm finally ended on the 22nd of June, and as from the 23rd, the DUKWs were once more able to resume unloading operations.

Arromanches during the storm.

A floating causeway overturned by the storm.

The beach at Arromanches in 1944 and seventy years later.

On the American side, the harbour at St. Laurent was far from complete and was highly vulnerable. To facilitate landing, the Americans had left additional gaps in the breakwater. The storm raged through these gaps, causing irreparable damage. The only jetty head to be in position in *Mulberry A* was destroyed by a group of 16 LCTs, which, whilst seeking shelter, collided with the jetty head. In addition, it appears that the Americans had taken less care than the British in placing and fixing the elements of the artificial harbour. The scuttled ships were not sufficiently close together and the Phoenix caissons were sunk in water which was too deep and were therefore quickly submerged by waves breaking over them. In addition, the Americans were over-optimistic regarding the need for anchoring, whilst the British had doubled the number of all their anchors.

At Arromanches, the artificial harbour valiantly withstood the force of the storm. Further advanced in its construction than *Mulberry A*, it had been protected by Phoenix caissons and by the Calvados Bank, a rocky area offshore which gave protection from bottom swell. Yet this did not totally prevent partial destruction, the shifting of the position of several caissons and a large number of craft being swept onto the shore (320 LCTs and numerous other craft). Everywhere, the rows of bombardons lost their anchors and, when they did not collide with and sink the Phoenix caissons, ended up on the beaches. At Utah beach and at the other beaches, half the smaller flat-bottomed craft were unusable for 36 to 48 hours. In the USA, during WW2, Major Ruppenthal stated that this storm was not among the most severe known to occur in the Channel, and that the weather conditions would prevent the use of the artificial harbours during the winter. He recalled that General Eisenhower, when faced with the extent of the storm damage, stressed the urgency of taking Cherbourg. For Admiral Kirk, if the storm had highlighted the weaknesses of the Mulberries, it had also demonstrated the importance of the *Gooseberries*, which provided a relatively sheltered area for the smaller craft, thus facilitating their unloading. This storm risked prejudicing the previous weeks' results. At *Mulberry A*, on 19th June, when the storm began, around half of the unloading objectives had been achieved. In the American Sector, 8,300 tonnes of supplies, 3,000 vehicles and 17,750 men had already been unloaded. From the next day, after the storm, the figures fell to only 1,000 tonnes, 738 vehicles and 3,300 men. Certain types of ammunition began to run short at a time when the 7th Corps started to launch its attack on Cherbourg.

The devastated *Mulberry A* installations the day after the storm.

In addition, the 1st U.S. Army decided to beach 8 ships loaded with ammunition and gave orders to the unloading units to give priority to ammunition and petrol. Little by little, *Mulberry B* was able to resume its operations. During the storm, the unloading of ammunition was hindered; however, as early as the 22nd of June, 1,200 of the 1,500 tonnes required by the British troops had been successfully unloaded.

In Normandy, after this great storm, which shattered both the hopes and plans of the Allies, just as it had devastated shipping (more than 800 vessels were blown on to the shore), all the harbour elements that were in the course of being towed across the Channel on the 19th of June were lost. Those which arrived on the 20th and 21st were severely damaged. The British and Americans had to get back to work. Since the capture of Cherbourg was believed to be imminent, *Mulberry A* was abandoned, although it could have been repaired in a few weeks. The destruction of Phoenix caissons was catastrophic. Twenty of the thirty caissons had been smashed by the force of the storm. Those that could be recovered were sent to *Mulberry B*. The remaining Phoenix units were to assist the unloading of the ships that were driven ashore over the following days. Only the shelter-jetty built of caissons was able to continue to offer shelter to the smaller landing craft. However, on the 23rd of June, unloading with DUKWs and ferries resumed and, the same day, 3,733 tonnes reached land. After the storm, activity at *Mulberry B* resumed. The east LST quay was the last to enter into service on the 17th of July.

Irreparable damage at *Mulberry A*.

THE HARBOURS' LAST DAYS

Present-day view of the bay of Arromanches.
Matthieu Barrabé – www.airstudio.fr.

Protected by the *Gooseberries*, the various beaches continued to contribute to resupplying the troops, either by transferring the supplies onto DUKWs or by beaching coasters. At Omaha, it became evident that the rocks were friable and a fleet of bulldozers set about making the beach suitable for the simultaneous beaching of a large number of ships which unloaded their cargoes directly onto lorries.

At the beginning of August, Supreme Allied Headquarters decided to continue using the artificial harbour at Arromanches for as long as the weather would allow, and therefore rejected the British Headquarters' proposal to use Cherbourg as soon as Brest was liberated. At the same time, it was decided to strengthen the harbour, in particular, by increasing the number of Phoenix caissons, so that it could operate during the winter.

Vestiges of "Beetles" grounded on the beach at Arromanches, opposite the D-Day Museum.

In September, General Gale, from the SHAEF, underlined the urgency of this reinforcement programme, noting that though Cherbourg had been taken two months earlier, it had not been possible to provide a berth for a single Liberty Ship (Liberty Ships were capable of transporting over 7,000 tonnes of supplies, i.e., three times the capacity of the largest coasters). With the capture of Antwerp on the 4th of September and Le Havre on the 12th, the lack of port facilities for unloading was about to come to an end. Moreover, the measures needed to make the harbour safe for use in winter were costly and the deterioration of the roads in the hinterland required considerable repair work.

By mid-October, Montgomery's 21st Army Group was anxious to recover its personnel and mobile port equipment which remained at Arromanches, so as to be able to re-equip the recently liberated Belgian ports (with the exception of Antwerp which was only able to reopen on the 26th of November). At this time, *Mulberry B* was only being used to discharge American Liberty Ships and for the transit of reserve supplies. The deterioration of the roads in the hinterland, coupled with the low capacity of the railway which served a port some 20km from there, led earlier decisions to be reconsidered and, on the 16th of October, a SHAEF conference ordered for the preparations to render harbour suitable for winter operations to be stopped and for the spare Phoenix and various other items to be transferred to Le Havre, which was operational from the 9th of October. Nevertheless, the unloading of supplies continued until the 31st of the month and torpedo boats went on using the harbour for as long as the weather permitted. Everything that could be removed was recovered, with the exception of one floating jetty reserved for U.S. ships and which operated until the 19th of November, when Omaha ceased unloading operations. The harbour was then abandoned.

Then followed the opening of Belgian and Dutch ports which were much closer to Montgomery's 21st Army battle zone and also to Nancy, where the American 3rd Army had established its advanced base. In addition, for supplies unloaded in Normandy, the rail links to the east could only handle 10,000 tonnes per day (whereas 20,000 tonnes were unloaded), hence the need to use a large fleet of lorries. The use of Antwerp considerably reduced the distance between the logistics bases and the front lines and did away with

This picture was taken upon the closure of Arromanches artificial harbour.

the complicated logistic system known as the Red Ball Express (this system consisted in reserving certain roads for military traffic. These one-way roads, starting from the Normandy beaches, went via Chartres, from where one route passed through Soissons and the other through Arcis-sur-Aube. Supplies followed these roads in a continuous stream, day and night).

The deterioration of the roads in Arromanches and the surrounding area took place because of the incessant traffic over four months. It had been a constant worry for those responsible for the area and the steps taken had proved inadequate, given the number of vehicles in circulation. The silting up of the Arromanches harbour caused sandbanks to appear here and there whilst at other points, the structures were settling into the seabed, causing the breakwaters and the quays to make unforeseeable movements. Designed to operate only during the ninety days of summer, the harbour had not only withstood use for a much longer period, but its contribution to supplying the troops had also been considerable.

This picture gives a good idea of the size of the elements that comprised the harbour. It shows a platform extension.

A balance sheet

In detail, these deliveries to the beaches were broken down as follows:

- From 6th to 19th June, the British beaches allowed the unloading within the shelter of the Gooseberries of 81,000 tonnes, 50,400 vehicles and 284,000 men. Of the three Anglo-Canadian *Gooseberries*, Courseulles was the most efficient, processing an average daily load of 1,028 tonnes of freight.

- Designed to unload 6,000 tonnes per day as from the 20th of June, *Mulberry B* processed a daily average of 3,800 tonnes. On the 16th of August, 9,513 tonnes of freight were unloaded – a record. A grand total of 690,900 tonnes of material were brought to shore from the 12th of June to the 19th of November 1944, the date the artificial harbour was officially closed. Although its yield was below forecasts, it enabled the British troops to be correctly provided with supplies and for thousands of wounded to be evacuated in excellent conditions.

Despite the capture of Antwerp on the 4th of September, it was impossible
to use it as a logistics base until the 28th of November, the day the seizure of Walcheren finally opened up access to this large port. Thus, during this vital period of the campaign, the supply lines, particularly for the Americans, were reliant on Cherbourg, Arromanches and the Normandy beaches.

At Christmas 1944, the dismantling of Arromanches began. The bridging units were to be used to replace bridges which had been destroyed, hence economising on the use of Bailey bridges which had been allocated to such use. Some refloated caissons were to replace sections of the sea wall at Walcheren which had been damaged by Allied bombing. After Germany's surrender, the British Army handed over to the French 183 steel sections of floating jetties which, from 1945 to 1948, permitted the rebuilding of around 60 large civil engineering structures.

The phenomenal deployment of logistics, here on Omaha Beach.

THE D-DAY MUSEUM

Matthieu Barrabé – www.airstudio.fr

Matthieu Barrabé – www.airstudio.fr

Come and discover the new D-Day Museum in Arromanches. Composed of seven sequences, the museum offers an insight into the incredible technological challenge involved in the construction of the artificial harbour. Visitors are first taken to a cinema, where a film explaining the various museum areas along the tour is screened.